Mindful Thoughts

Jennifer Jones

Published by New Generation Publishing in 2020

First Edition

ISBN 978-1-80031-545-7

www.newgeneration-publishing.com

New Generation Publishing

Thank You

Gratitude

To all who have taken the time to purchase and read this book. To my special family, who have supported me through thick and thin.

With much admiration, love, and gratitude Em & Bill, who played a big part in my life. Lotte Mikkelsen, with her bountiful energy and hard working ethos, towards helping others, with lots of Laughter and Joy. James Underwood who is an amazing Chiropractor, who looks after bones as well as your well being, helping you achieve more than you every thought possible. Kate Cant, a very good friend who helped with her kindness to make, this book materialise.

Why I Wrote, Mindful Thoughts

I have written this book because, after many years of reading, and using Quotes, Mantras, Slogans and Phrases throughout my life, I wanted to create new ones, that would be uplifting, healing, comforting and humorous and give encouragement for oneself. Many people have heard, used or seen Quotes, Mantras, Slogans and Phrases, that are used in some form or another, and will be continued to be used.

I wrote Mindful Thoughts to enable us to look at things from a different perspective, helping with our internal thoughts and feelings.

There are a variety of mind thoughts in this book, some personal, observational, and deeply thoughtful, to be also totally honest, a few that are just, right out there.

I know from personal experience it is not always the easiest thing to talk about your thoughts and feelings.

Mindful Thoughts have so many different Quotes, Mantras, Slogans and Phrases to choose from. I'm sure you will find a favourite or two.

Mindful Thoughts

1. Freedom fills you with everything. Lets you do anything. Freedom can never stop you from dying, so live your life.

2. I am in the right place, at the right time, for right now.

3. Life can sometimes feel like a bitter pill, so take laughter as your liquid and it will dissipate a lot easier.

4. My thoughts, and dreams, are like the wind, they materialise everywhere.

5. If you visited my mind. How long would you stay?

6. I feel excited, when I don't know why.

7. I love myself inside and out, because I am me.

8. Love sometimes can seem like taking in someone else's emotional baggage, and to help deal with it, try leaving it at the airport.

9. When life hands you drama, just hand it right back.

10. It's not how young or how old you are. It's just how you are.

11. Have you been dealt lemons? Then just change the fruit.

12. Being still is being silent. Being silent enables us to listen. Listening enables us to understand. Understanding is gaining knowledge. Gaining knowledge is obtaining wisdom. Gaining wisdom leads to growth. Growth leads to expansion. Expand.

13. Connect with me on a vibrational high and take me to places no universal equilibrium can.

14. When you look at me, my mind is continually in different states of thoughts, feelings and analytical processing.

15. When I explore my own truths, allow others to explore theirs.

16. If there are only two sides to every story. Then that is all there is.

17. You would not recognise me, when I smile.

18. You have all the answers.

19. The final decision I make, will always be mine.

20. When you are at rock bottom, take a good look at that rock, you will see more than you think.

21. Step into my shoes, try and not to fall flat on your face.

22. No one will ever know me. Like me. But you can try!

23. I can see the drop, I can feel the drop, I can hear the drop, but it's not raining.

24. Forgiving, is giving me back my freedom and letting whatever it is, go.

25. Time goes with money, time goes without money. Enjoy your time.

26. I am happy when it is sunny, I am happy when it is raining, I am happy when it is snowing. I'm happy with any weather.

27. If I don't listen to you and you don't listen to me, how are we going to learn?

28. If time is the greatest healer. Then all I need, is time.

29. When I reach out my hand to you. I know that you're not always going to take it. But I will leave it there for you anyway.

30. Sometimes I need to be loud, to drown out the chatter in my head.

31. Why do we have to wait? Because extraordinary things happen.

32. Pain is a feeling to remember, for a very good reason. That we have to do something about it, whether, physically, emotional or mentally.

33. If you inspire me, so that I can inspire others. Thank you for your inspiration.

34. When the universe speaks to you, listen, and it can take you all the way.

35. I bring myself back to the now, just by focusing on my breath.

36. Listen to the silence, and it will show you, how much more you can hear.

37. One size does not fit all, neither was it meant to.

38. Dance to the rhythm of someone else's beat, and you will feel discontentment. Dance to your own beat and you will feel joy.

39. Change your face today – with just a smile.

40. You can always change your direction in life – be like a compass.

41. Book me on a plane to nowhere, so I can go everywhere.

42. Every time I hear a car toot, I think of a loved one.

43. Relaxation is for everyone, even me!

44. To make things brighter in your life, increase your wattage, with lots of positivity.

45. Do it now. Do it tomorrow, do it whenever, as long as you do.

46. If you had the opportunity to do it, would you?

47. Time passes slowly, time passes fast, time passes whether you use it or abuse it, time will pass.

48. When a squirrel hides their nuts, they are not worried where they hide them, on many occasions they will not even find them.

49. I unshackle my attachments, because it allows me free flow.

50. I worry about everyone, except me.

51. There are many paths to the same destination it doesn’t matter if you find yourself on a different one.

52. Take a step closer, and not a step back.

53. When I forgive. My mind, and my body will reap all the rewards.

54. Feeling lost? You will always find somewhere?

55. If our love lasts a lifetime, we were the perfect match, and if it didn’t, we were still the perfect match.

56. Let’s start the day positive, in every way.

57. It is so important to remember yourself, and how important you really are.

58. Don’t rely on others to fulfil your happiness, find it for yourself.

59. When we see the same thing, our interpretations will always be different.

60. When I can forgive you. I can forgive myself.

61. My glass is always full, because I like it full.

62. My memories will always be stored in my mind.

63. Don't control me with fear, encourage me with love.

64. If I was a pair of socks, I would be an odd pair, because odd is amazing.

65. Music touches my soul with loving arms and holds me tight, not ever wanting to let go of me.

66. Separating was the best solution. It finally enabled us.

67. Can I ever love another? I can and I will, when the time is right.

68. I am beautiful with or without.

69. When I see myself in someone else. Who needs help, I give so much more.

70. Don't misconstrue my silence. When silence is what I need at this time.

71. Please and thank you, make a great couple.

72. When I stare into the mirror, only beauty is staring back at me.

73. Just because it is, it does not have to be.

74. The minimal can be enough.

75. We all speak the same language, when in love.

76. Speak less and listen more.

77. Embrace your uniqueness and individuality, don't let it go to waste.

78. Every type of meditation is powerful.

79. I have amazing experiences, through learning and growth, so I can contribute, to enhancing this beautiful world.

80. We are all connected, so tap in and connect by turning your tap on.

81. GRATEFUL – Giving Real Appreciation To Exercise Forever Undulating Love.

82 Words can lift you up. Words can cut you down. Choose words wisely.

83 Knowing the truth can be painful, living a lie can be destructive.

84 When the face in the mirror stares back at me, I may see something different. But I love what I see.

85 Don't deny yourself.

86 It is me, I am loving first, so that I can give you much more.

87 CHANGE – Celebrate Having Another New Great Experience.

88 With perfect health, you hold the key to unlock the benefits.

89 If you can't question everything, how can you find the answers?

90 If you had the opportunity to choose your life? Why not start now?

91 If peace lives within you, allow peace to spill out of you.

92 If I don’t know? How can I make things right?

93 As difficult as it may seem, in a negative situation there is always a positive that will arrive.

94 I enjoy you, all of you.

95 Thinking outside the box, is necessary to finding so much more.

96 I allow my light to shine. To attract those who would like to see clearer.

97 My life is unique. Is yours?

98 When you make space, you make room.

99 If I beat to the sound of my own drum and you beat to the sound of your own drum, we can make sweet drum beats.

100 When there is total balance in all areas of your life, life in all areas are balanced.

101 The most important vibration to be aware of, is your own. When we fill our bodies and thoughts with vibrations. We can connect to the flow of the universe's vibrations.

102 Don't wait for someone to buy you flowers, just buy your own.

103 You might be surprised at the little things that I don't know about you.

104 If you can make time for this, then you can definitely make time for that.

105 There are opportunities everywhere, all you have to do is just notice them, they are everywhere.

106 Enjoy your time, because time wants to enjoy you.

107 I didn't have much time. "But you did."

108 If you can't be your own spokesperson. Who will be?

109 When you are close to me, you make me feel warm, when you are far away you still make me feel warm.

110 Let me carry you. So you have the strength to carry someone else.

111 When it should be. When it isn’t. Why can’t it be?

112 I place my heart in your hands for as long as you care to hold it.

113 Emotions can be like thin twigs, with a little bit of pressure, they can easily snap.

114 Darkness does not always make things visible, but seeing it in the light always can.

115 Look past what is in front of you, then you might see a lot more.

116 My heart is bruised. But bruises fade.

117 Time does not go back, time can only go forward.

118 My home can be anywhere as long as I am there.

119 An empty space gives me room to grow and flow.

120 My time is my time and your time is yours.

121 It is not your job to figure me out. It's my job.

122 I may be scared of the truth. But the truth will not scare me.

123 Play to my strengths, and I will work on my weaknesses.

124 If fear was my friend, I would get to know it very well. So there will be nothing to fear, because I know fear very well.

125 I would like to be alone. I would like to be with family. I would like to be with friends. When I would like to be.

126 I face challenges every day. Because I have to.

127 I may be scared to hear the truth. But the truth is what I need.

128 When I say yes, but I really mean no. Give me the courage to say what I really mean.

129 My business is my business and your business is your business, don't get the two confused.

130 I have not gone to make you sad. I have not gone to make you cry. I have not gone to cause you pain. I have not gone to disrupt your life. I have gone because death needed me as much as you did. Thank you for the memories.

131 Negative situations can end, with incredible outcomes.

132 Everything always starts from nothing.

www.ingramcontent.com/pod-product-compliance
Ingram Content Group UK Ltd.
Pitfield, Milton Keynes, MK11 3LW, UK
UKHW041843200726
13854UKWH00005BA/1896
9 781800 315457